A College Girl's Guide

To Living in Faith

Table of Contents

College. What a time to be alive! Rules are limited, life is off to a new start, you become a "blank slate," you can meet new people (or hide in your room), you can take exciting classes, and eat loads and loads of pizza! Freedom is everywhere, but responsibilities sneak up. How do you manage this exciting new part of life, while still maintaining a Godly heart? How do you choose the will of God when all it feels like you are doing is eating, sleeping, studying, and having fun? Does living a Christian life mean that you have to suddenly change your whole schedule to fit God in? Do you have to stop doing certain things you love to make time for God or make a place for him in your heart? And how can you find purpose in the mundane aspects of student life? These are questions that I've asked myself many times, and I have heard others ask, as well. In this study, we will dive deeper into these questions and many others. Be prepared to challenge yourself as you learn and grow in the areas this devotional covers.

Chapter 1: Focus

What *is* focus?

Imagine getting ready for a big game. You're focused and ready to win. Maybe it's a soccer match, a basketball game, a race, or anything else. Whatever it is, you're focused in on the task ahead and you're ready to do your best. This type of energy could be called *focus*. When we are focused, we are determined to do something. We put our energy into it, and we don't get distracted by other things. When we are not focused, it messes up our chances of being as effective as we want to be.

How big of a deal is focusing?

Sometimes, it's not that big of a deal! Not everything in life requires 100% focus. The problem comes when focus is not applied to God. We step out of focus because we have too many things going on, because life is too busy, because "it's ok, I can talk to God tonight...or maybe tomorrow." We don't have special brain superpowers. Most of us cannot devote an equal amount of time, effort, determination, and focus to multiple things. We have to choose where to put our energy.

- How often are we putting energy and effort into what God wants us to do?
- How much time do we spend trying to hear His still, small voice, and letting God influence our actions?
- How much do we meditate on His Word, and let it speak to us?
- How much do we pray?

We get busy; it's inevitable. We have to focus on things like jobs, school, family, friends, etc. We have to put effort into multiple areas of life. **But as we live on earth, our driving force for every action, reaction, thought, and decision should be our *focus* on the Kingdom of God.** If we are devoted to do the will of God, to bring glory to Him, and to see His Kingdom expanded, then our relationship with Him is the primary thing we should put our thoughts and efforts into.

How to avoid distraction

There are some simple ways to get rid of big distractions on our lives. For example, how often do you wake up and scroll through your phone for two minutes, which then becomes 15 minutes, and then turns into 30 minutes? We let time slip away by doing things that don't truly matter. It's ok to scroll through your phone, but how much of that time could be spent productively?

- Try tracking your phone activity for one week. How often were you on it per day? How much time did you spend on social media?
- Are there ways that you can reduce your phone time and replace it with something like a devotional, or by praying?
- Keep a journal and write down your thoughts, concerns, prayers, etc. It's a lot easier to focus when you are physically writing something, as opposed to just thinking.
- Remember that little changes make a big difference. You won't wake up one day with laser focus. Start small and continue making changes.

The enemy knows how powerful our minds are. He knows how much we can accomplish when we put our minds to something! So, he is going to try to do everything he can do distract us. When he gets into our minds, he can influence our actions, behaviors, world views, attitudes, and so much more. He will put things in our lives every day to stress us out. He will try to cause us to slip up. BUT if our *focus* doesn't lie on these things, they won't knock us down!

Romans 12:2, "Do not be conformed to this world, but be transformed by the renewal of your MIND..."

Colossians 3:2, "Set your MIND on things above, not things on the earth."

A Daily Effort

When we decide to put more focus on God, it is not going to be super easy. **You will mess up sometimes.** However, instead of getting discouraged, be encouraged! Each day is a new opportunity to focus on God. Remember that change takes time! You have to be determined to change your life and to do it every day. God will honor your efforts, even if they start out as small. *Remember that as time goes by, try to challenge yourself.* Focusing on God may not be easy, but it will be so beneficial.

Set Your Mind

We set our *MINDS* on God. We choose to surrender ourselves for Him daily, to listen to Him *first,* to put our relationship with Him first, to serve Him first, to talk to Him first, to seek His counsel first. We have to make a conscious decision to run after God--to align ourselves with His Word. We don't procrastinate, we don't avoid, we don't run away...we focus our attention on Him. Our minds are capable of so much, and when our minds are on GOD, our entire lives will be positively impacted! The things that seem like such a big deal suddenly won't seem as important. The things that stress us out won't affect us as they did before! This is because they aren't what we focus on anymore.

When we set our minds on God, we see everything else on this earth with an eternal perspective. Our "heavenly" mindset influences the way we see things, instead of the circumstances in our lives dictating how we see things. Our thoughts become fruitful. We think on what is *true, noble, right, lovely, pure, admirable, excellent, and praiseworthy (Philippians 4:8).*

- Write down the top five things that distract you the most:
  - 1.
  - 2.
  - 3.
  - 4.
  - 5.
- What are some ways that you can spend less time focusing on your distractions?

- Do you think any of these distractions are put into your life by the enemy? Why/why not?

- Start small. What is one thing you will do to begin focusing more on God?

- Matthew 6:33, "But seek first the kingdom of God and His righteousness, and all these things will be added to you."
  - Thoughts:

- Phillipians 4:8, "Finally, brothers, whatever is true, whatever is honorable, whatever is just, whatever is pure, whatever is lovely, whatever is commendable, if there is any excellence, if there is anything worthy of praise, think about these things."
    - Thoughts:

- Matthew 6:24, "No one can serve two masters, for either he will hate the one and love the other, or he will be devoted to the one and despise the other. You cannot serve God and money."
    - Thoughts:

- Proverbs 16:3, "Commit your work to the Lord, and your plans will be established."
    - Thoughts:

Chapter 2: Purpose

Do you ever wonder why you are here? Do you think about why you were created, or what you are created to do? College is a time of discovery, and a time where you are supposed to choose what you want to do for your career. Certainly you can find purpose and meaning in your job, but do you ever wonder if there is, or could be, more to your life?

God's Purpose for Your Life

Matthew 28:19-20, "Go therefore and make disciples of all nations, baptizing them in the name of the Father and of the Son and of the Holy Spirit, teaching them to observe all that I have commanded you. And behold, I am with you always, to the end of the age."

This verse captures what God desires that all Christians do. He has sent the Holy Spirit so that we can:

1. GO
2. Make disciples (of ALL nations)
3. Baptize in the name of the Father, the Son, and the Holy Spirit
4. Teach all that God has commanded
5. Know that God is always with you

We as Christians are called to go out into all the earth and share the Gospel (which is the message that Jesus lived on this earth as 100% man and 100% God, died for our sins, arose from the grave, and has sent the Holy Spirit to be with us today). What does this mean, then, if you are a college student who is stuck in one location? You probably don't have money to travel, and how do you even *start* making disciples?

Fulfilling God's Purpose Where You Are

I believe that God calls people to go outside of their comfort zones. God will place a desire in some people's hearts to share the Gospel in distant areas. Not all of us, however, have to travel far in order to make disciples and spread the Gospel. If every Christian was traveling to share the Word of God, who would share it in all the places left behind? Who would share the Word of God to their neighbors, friends, and relatives?

You can spread the Word of God by *living out what you believe.* Whether you are studying to become a doctor, a lawyer, a teacher, a counselor, a sports therapist, or anything else, you can live as God has called all Christians to live.

Matthew 5:13-16, "You are the salt of the earth, but if salt has lost its taste, how shall its saltiness be restored? It is no longer good for anything except to be thrown out and trampled under people's feet. You are the light of the world. A city set on a hill cannot be hidden. Nor do people light a lamp and put it under a basket, but on a stand, and it gives light to all in the house. In the same way, let your light shine before others, so that they may see your good works and give glory to your Father who is in heaven."

Ask God daily to help you live the way He wants you to live. Ask Him for the Fruit of the Spirit. The "Fruit of the Spirit" is a metaphor for positive things in your life that come out of *growing* with God. When a fruit tree grows, it is fed and fed and fed with water, and grows slowly. It eventually produces fruit that others can see and eat from. In the same way, as you are "fed" by reading the Word of God, God pours His nourishment into your life like water. If you are nourished continually, you will grow little by little until you are a beautiful "tree" that has "fruit" (which are signs that God has worked in your life and has grown you). The Fruit of the Spirit, found in Galatians 5:22-23, are:

- Love
- Joy
- Peace
- Patience
- Kindness
- Goodness
- Faithfulness
- Gentleness
- Self-Control

When others see these attributes that you have, they will notice you are different. As you grow in relationship with those around you, and continue displaying the fruit of the Spirit, others may ask you questions. They may ask you why you act the way that you do. Some people may not like you, but don't let this hurt you. Your purpose is to continue your relationship with the Lord, and to continue growing in Him. Your purpose is not to please other people. There will always be those who don't like you, but whether you realize it or not, other people will be looking up to you and watching you. It may take time, but eventually you will see people come to know the Lord, simply because of how you outwardly display your own love for Him.

Service

Think about this question: *If someone used the word **always** to describe your life, what would they say you are **always doing?***

Matthew 23:11, "The greatest among you will be your servant."

When we serve others, we are actually serving God. God loves it when we serve others, because we are doing what Jesus would have done. We are loving those around us, no matter who they are. We are putting others before ourselves, and honoring God by doing so.

Service can be small things that no one sees. The small things are actually the big things that make a difference. When you may feel insignificant, you are actually making a big impact. Imagine this scenario: you see a girl who always appears a little lonely. She looks sad, and doesn't want to talk to anyone. Perhaps you pass her everyday as you walk to class. You smile at her, and she looks at you, but never smiles back. Every day, though, you show patience and love and you continue to smile at her as you walk past her. One day she stops you and asks you why you smile at her. You can explain that you wanted to make her day better, and wanted her to know that someone cares for her. After several little encounters with her, she describes to you a difficult situation she is going through, and how she felt alone and didn't want to be close to anyone. She ignored your smile because she didn't want to let anyone in. You now have the opportunity to talk to her, grow a relationship with her and share the love of God. It all started with a smile!

Our attitude when it comes to serving the Lord and living for Him should be: wherever, whenever, and however you need me to be used, <u>USE ME.</u>

- What are you *always* doing that you can do to make an impact on this world?

- Think about some people that you know. How can you shine God's love to them?

- For each fruit of the Spirit, write down ways to express the "fruit" in your life.
  - Love:

  - Joy:

  - Peace:

  - Patience:

  - Kindness:

  - Goodness:

  - Gentleness:

  - Faithfulness:

  - Self-control:

YOUR Individual, Unique Purpose

The general purpose for all of us is to serve God, to make disciples, to make His name known, to baptize, to teach, and to have a relationship with Him. However, *how* you will make disciples and *in what way* you will make His name known is unique. You are created one-of-a-kind. You were born with characteristics different than those around you. Think about your desires, your strengths, and your weaknesses. What do you find joy in doing? What are you good at (and you can't say *nothing,* because everyone can be good at something)? What do you definitely *not* enjoy doing?

God has put desires in your heart that He wants to use. The closer you get with God, the more He will reveal these things to you. Maybe you already know! The things that you love to do could be the areas in which God wants you to serve. You are different than anyone else. **God will use the characteristics He has placed inside of you if you let Him.** He will use you in ways that you didn't think were possible. He will grow you, and you will learn more about yourself and about Him. He will reveal to you the good things about you. He has already given you everything you need to serve Him. You don't have to be "called" by God in a magical way. If you are a Christian, you are automatically called by God to serve Him. If you want to understand more of your individual purpose, however, you have desire a relationship with Him. You have to *focus* your attention on Him and His Word.

- Think about what you love to do. Write down some of your interests and hobbies here:

- Can you think of any ways that you can serve God in these areas? If you can't, start praying about them. Ask God to show you ways that you can serve Him in these areas.

- What are your strengths? List some below (<u>Anything...</u>if you can make an amazing cup of coffee, write that down).

- Ephesians 2:10, "For we are God's handiwork, created in Christ Jesus to do good works, which God prepared in advance for us to do."
  - ○ Thoughts:

- James 1:17, "Every good and perfect gift is from above, coming down from the Father of the heavenly lights, who does not change like shifting shadows."
  - ○ Thoughts:

- 1 Corinthians 12:5-6, "There are different kinds of service, but the same Lord. There are different kinds of working, but in all of them and in everyone it is the same God at work.
  - Thoughts:

- Proverbs 20:5, "The purposes of a person's heart are deep waters, but one who has insight draws them out."
  - Thoughts:

- Ephesians 2:10, "For we are God's handiwork, created in Christ Jesus to do good works, which God prepared in advance for us to do."
  - Thoughts:

Chapter 3: Identity

Identity is something that I have struggled with most of my life. I sometimes have trouble accepting who I am. When I was younger, I didn't know how to get over this. I would have times where I would get down on myself, because I realized I was "stuck" inside a person that I didn't like. My mind was so focused on myself and what I didn't like about myself. I didn't look at the positive attributes that I have, because I couldn't see them. Finding your identity can be extremely beneficial in your own life and in your spiritual life. Finding your identity can open up amazing opportunities and can inspire you to serve God the way in which you were created.

Who Am I?

Think about who you are for a second. What do you act like? What do you look like? What are your interests? What do you think about? Like we discovered in the chapter on purpose, you are uniquely designed and crafted for a special purpose. However, *you* need to understand that about yourself. If you don't believe that you are created by God in a beautiful way, you will not realize your full potential.

Every single person has weaknesses. No one is even close to perfect. Actually, I think that it is important to understand what weaknesses and faults you have. You may have a laundry list of things you don't like about yourself. You may only have a couple things that you can think of. Whatever the case may be, you should know that you are flawed and that on your own, you will mess up. You will not be able to do all that God wants you to do, or be who he wants you to be, if your identity is based off of what you like or don't like about yourself.

Christ Jesus died so that all of your sin, shame, faults, and regrets can be gone. All that you have to do is accept that He is God, that He came to the earth to live a perfect, sinless life, and that He died as the ultimate sacrifice so that all of your sins may be forgiven. He rose again three days later, and left us with the Holy Spirit as our helper. Now we, as daughters of Christ, do not have to worry about our sins or our faults. We simply surrender to God, and ask that He shape us into who He wants us to be. We ask God to use our gifts and bring out the good in us. We ask God for wisdom so that we can see the good that He has placed in us. Daily we ask God to forgive us and to grow us.

Your identity is not a sum total of all of your characteristics, strengths, and weaknesses. Rather, your identity is founded on the fact that the God who created all of heaven and earth came to this earth and died so that you may be saved. You are a daughter of the Most High. He created you and your identity is founded in Him. You are a princess; a daughter of the King. You have been set apart and created uniquely. God _will_ use you. He needs you and has a specific purpose for your life, and that is who you are and why you are here. As you grow in your walk with the Lord, you will discover more of His plan for you. Step by step His plan will unfold as you walk with Him and go where He leads you.

How do I know where God is leading me?

Sometimes, God speaks in audible ways. God speaks through visions, dreams, signs, etc. Other times, it is hard to hear God and to understand what He is saying. To discover where God is leading you, you need to pray and ask Him. Your everyday life should consist of conversations with God through prayer. It is also impossible to understand what God wants you to do without also reading His Word. This doesn't mean you have to read pages and pages every day. It is really important to meditate on the Word of God and study the Bible closely. If you focus on one verse for the whole day, that can be powerful. Let Him speak to you by what He has already written down for you to hear.

You are Not Defined by Your Past

Your identity in Christ is <u>not</u> defined by your past. Whatever sin you may have gone through, or still struggle with, Christ has forgiven and has set you free. Now, you do not have to think of your past mistakes. You don't have to feel like you are undeserving of love, because God loves you and accepts you. You don't have to feel like a bad person, because your identity is not rooted in what you have done. Your identity is rooted in the fact that you are God's prized possession, and your goal should be to encourage others by living this out. What you think about, you will say. What you say, you will do. What you do will become who you are. Thus, think about Christ. Think about your relationship with Him, and how He has made you new. Do not dwell on your struggles or your past. Think about perfect love, and a perfect God that you will meet one day. Think about living for Him and watching the excitement unfold! Think about being an example to others around you and sharing Christ's love!

- Think about how you would describe your identity. Write some things down that come to mind:

- Does your identity (how you see yourself) line up with who God has called you to be...that is, a daughter and someone who serves Him?

- What are some things that you can do every day that remind you of who you are in Christ?

- Does your past ever hold you back from becoming a "new person" with Christ?

- What are some things that you want God to change in your life? In what ways do you believe God has already gifted you?

- John 1:12, "Yet to all who did receive Him, to those who believed in His name, He gave the right to become children of God—"
    - ○ Thoughts:

- Romans 6:6, "For we know that our old self was crucified with Him so that the body ruled by sin might be done away with, that we should no longer be slaves to sin—"
    - ○ Thoughts:

- 1 Peter 2:9, "But you are a chosen people, a royal priesthood, a holy nation, God's special possession, that you may declare the praises of Him who called you out of darkness into his wonderful light."
    - ○ Thoughts:

Chapter 4: Trust

Trust is not an easy task. To trust someone requires laying down your defenses and becoming vulnerable. Depending on your history of trusting others, you may or may not trust anyone in your life. People who have been there for you and haven't let you down are extremely special. However, we are all human and being perfect is impossible. People are not foolproof, and they are not the best thing to put your trust in. You make mistakes, so it is hard to trust yourself, too. Who can you trust? This answer you probably could have guessed based on the previous chapters. In short, you can only truly trust God. God is the *only One* who will never make mistakes. He is the One who holds all of the wisdom and knowledge. He has created you, the earth, and everything in it.

Letting Go

As I have journeyed from my teenage years into my twenties, I have noticed a growing anxiety that I have. I worry about my life all the time. I'm worried about how my day will go. I worry about the little things, like how I am going to get my studying done or how I'm going to put together my daily schedule. I also worry about bigger things, like what my life will look like in twenty years, if I will be making an impact, if I will still have my good friends, etc. I worry about losing control of my life. I am the type of person that likes to plan and control my life, and when it doesn't go my way, I try to fix it. This can be a strength of mine in certain circumstances, but it also makes me stubborn when it comes to "letting go."

The reality is that I do not need to worry. I don't have to try to control my life situation. I don't have to stress over every little detail, everything that *might* go wrong, and every worry I may have. As long as I am actively seeking after God, I can have peace.

Think about that word for a minute. *Peace.*

Have you ever truly felt peace?

I struggle to let go because I lack trust. I am worried that things will not go *my way*. I'm afraid that *I won't* be comfortable. I don't like not having a plan, so *I get afraid* of trusting God and walking blindly into my future. I want to do what God wants me to do, but I want an outline from Him. I want Him to give me my life line-by-line, so I can know what to expect. I want to see all of the challenges beforehand instead of just going through them. I want to see which decisions I should make and which I shouldn't. I worry and worry until I meditate on the simple truth: God is in control.

God is a good God. He knows all of your fears and He sees your entire life. He won't show you what's ahead all the time, because He wants you to live your life. He wants you to treat every day as if it were your last...serving Him with all that you have because you never know what's next. He wants to see your face when you rejoice in a triumph. He wants to hold your hand when you're going through a struggle. He wants to be your guide, not your fortune teller. He wants you to *trust Him* and choose to walk with Him. He is the God who created all things. He created everything around you and He created you, too. He can make anything happen *in an instant.* He will not let you down and He will <u>never</u> leave you. The God who holds the entire world in His hands hears you and cares for you. Who better to put all of your trust, all of your hope, and all of your affections in?

Relationships are founded on trust. How can you have a good relationship if you are constantly doubting your friend or partner? In the same way, how can you have a good relationship with God if you are constantly doubting what He can do? *When we lay down what **we think we want,** God give us **what we need.*** We have to give up what we think we want our life to look like and trust God to handle it. This doesn't mean that we have an excuse to sit back, be lazy, and let life pass us by! We need to actively seek God and He will direct our desires, set up people for us to meet, guide our steps, and make it all come together. God may work in your life discreetly, and you will only be able to look back and see how He put your life together. God may also work obviously in your life, and you will be able to see exactly how He is helping you in the moment. No matter how God is working in your life, it is important to fully trust Him with your life. Even when life gets hard, trust that God is always with you and He is an *always faithful* God.

- Do you fully trust God with your life? If not, what are the hardest parts of your life to surrender control?

- Are you ever afraid of letting go? What are some verses from God's Word that can encourage you to let go (there will be some listed later in this chapter)?

- Are you open to doing whatever God has in store for you, even if it is hard?

- Letting go means following what God wants, not what you want. Are you willing to commit your whole life to the Lord, even if things don't happen exactly as you thought they would?

- Joshua 1:9, "Have I not commanded you? Be strong and courageous. Do not be afraid; do not be discouraged, for the LORD your God will be with you wherever you go."
    - Thoughts:

- Psalm 9:10, "Those who know your name trust in you, for you, LORD, have never forsaken those who seek you."
    - Thoughts:

- Psalm 13:5, "But I trust in your unfailing love; my heart rejoices in your salvation."
  - Thoughts:

- Proverbs 3:5-6, "Trust in the LORD with all your heart and lean not on your own understanding; in all your ways submit to him, and he will make your paths straight."
  - Thoughts:

- Proverbs 28:26, "Those who trust in themselves are fools, but those who walk in wisdom are kept safe."
  - Thoughts:

- Romans 15:13, "May the God of hope fill you with all joy and peace as you trust in him, so that you may overflow with hope by the power of the Holy Spirit."
  - Thoughts:

- Proverbs 16:3, "Commit to the Lord whatever you do,and he will establish your plans."
  - Thoughts:

- Psalm 143:8, "Let the morning bring me word of your unfailing love, for I have put my trust in you. Show me the way I should go, for to you I entrust my life."
  - Thoughts:

- Isaiah 43:2, "When you pass through the waters, I will be with you; and when you pass through the rivers, they will not sweep over you. When you walk through the fire, you will not be burned; the flames will not set you ablaze."
  - Thoughts:

- 2 Corinthians 5:7, "For we live by faith, not by sight."
  - Thoughts:

- Hebrews 13:5, "Keep your lives free from the love of money and be content with what you have, because God has said, "Never will I leave you; never will I forsake you."
  - Thoughts:

- Proverbs 16:20, "Whoever gives heed to instruction prospers, and blessed is the one who trusts in the Lord."
  - Thoughts:

- 1 John 4:16, "And so we know and rely on the love God has for us. God is love. Whoever lives in love lives in God, and God in them."
  - Thoughts:

Chapter 5: Watch Your Tongue

The tongue is a powerful tool that has more power than we think. The words that we say can either build people up or break them down. We have an ability to convey what we think through words. We can use words in ways that we want to, in order to get outcomes we desire. We can use words to ask questions and give answers. We use words every day, but how much of what we are saying really matters? Is what we are saying encouraging and kind?

Do Not Be a Fault Finder

It is incredibly easy to find faults in other people. Finding faults in others is especially easy when you are insecure in your own skin. When you are insecure, you compare yourself to others, and oftentimes try to bring others down to make yourself appear "better" than them. I'm saying this because I know from experience that this is the truth. I have seen it in my own life, and in the lives of others. I have insecurities, and sometimes it makes me feel better to compare myself to others by finding their faults and thinking "at least I don't have *that*" or, "at least I don't do *that.*"

This is an incredibly easy trap to get into. Thinking negatively of someone encourages gossip. Pretty soon, you have a skewed image of someone in your mind based off of the things that you don't like about them. In my high school and college experiences, I have witnessed and participated in gossip. The outcome of gossip was never pretty, and it has many negative consequences. Gossip also never made me feel any better about myself, but instead only made me more angry and critical towards others.

Why is it so easy to be a "fault finder?" This is because we operate out of pride, insecurity, and jealousy. Think about this...have you ever known a very critical person that you actually *enjoy* being around? Do they make you feel uplifted and happy? Proverbs 21:19 says, "better to live in a desert than with a quarrelsome and nagging wife." This verse may apply to spouses, but I believe it also applies to any close relationship that includes quarrels and nags. It is not good to be around people like this, but it is even worse to *be* someone like this.

How do you break out of the cycle of gossip, nagging, quarreling, and finding fault in others? It starts with focusing on who others *are,* not focusing on who they *are not.* It may be challenging at first, but changing the way you view others can also change your heart. As christians, it is especially critical that we look at the good in others and encourage them in this way. We can spread God's love through encouragement and uplifting words. Rather than judging others on what they do wrong or what they don't have, we should pray for them. We should also be the ones that make them feel loved and special, no matter how many things are wrong in their life.

God's Necessary Strength

Focusing on the good in others takes a tremendous effort. Focusing on the good in others also means that it is important not to participate in gossip, which only leads to negative outcomes. On our own, we cannot do this. The Holy Spirit is there to help us in our weaknesses, so that we can find the strength to help others. Instead of being fault finders, we can be hope dealers. Words are life. If you are constantly bringing others down with your words, even behind their backs, you are not encouraging them to become better people. These actions will also have a negative effect on you. It is necessary to ask God for strength and wisdom when it comes to dealing with others. The Holy Spirit will guide you and give you the words to say. As you focus on the good in others, you will see your mindset change. You will see how your own identity becomes grounded, and your life will change for the better.

Have you ever heard the phrase "if you don't have anything good to say, don't say anything at all"? This phrase should apply to our lives, especially when dealing with others. Before you speak, *think* about what you are saying. Is it true? Is it helpful? Does it display fruit of the Spirit (love, joy, peace, patience, etc.)? If not, is it even worth saying? Do you really want to use your words to bring other people down, even if you aren't talking directly to them? Watch your tongue and think about your words and the impact they have. Don't underestimate the power of what you say!

- Think about how much you gossip during the day. Is it a lot? A little? How can you focus on "holding your tongue?"

- Do you know people that bother you? How can you pray for them and find ways to encourage them, instead of being frustrated?

- Think about certain people in your life. Write down the positive things about them that you can focus on.

- Have you ever had something hurtful said to you? How did it make you feel?

- Make a plan to really take time to think about what you want to say before you say it. If you feel like you are getting caught up with other people who are starting gossip, don't participate. In fact, you can be the one who stands up for other people! You would be surprised in how people will look up to you for doing this.

- 1 Peter 3:10, "For, "Whoever would love life and see good days must keep their tongue from evil and their lips from deceitful speech."
  - Thoughts:

- Colossians 4:6, "Let your conversation be always full of grace, seasoned with salt, so that you may know how to answer everyone."
  - Thoughts:

- Ephesians 4:29, "Do not let any unwholesome talk come out of your mouths, but only what is helpful for building others up according to their needs, that it may benefit those who listen."
  - Thoughts:

- Proverbs 10:19, "Sin is not ended by multiplying words, but the prudent hold their tongues."
  - Thoughts:

- Proverbs 15:4, "The soothing tongue is a tree of life, but a perverse tongue crushes the spirit."
  - Thoughts:

- Matthew 15:11, "What goes into someone's mouth does not defile them, but what comes out of their mouth, that is what defiles them."
  - Thoughts:

- Proverbs 21:23, "Those who guard their mouths and their tongues keep themselves from calamity."
  - Thoughts:

- Proverbs 26:20, "Without wood a fire goes out; without a gossip a quarrel dies down."
  - Thoughts:

- Psalm 141:3, "Set a guard over my mouth, LORD; keep watch over the door of my lips."
  - Thoughts:

- James 1:19-26, "19 My dear brothers and sisters, take note of this: Everyone should be quick to listen, slow to speak and slow to become angry, 20 because human anger does not produce the righteousness that God desires. 21 Therefore, get rid of all moral filth and the evil that is so prevalent and humbly accept the word planted in you, which can save you. 22 Do not merely listen to the word, and so deceive yourselves. Do what it says. 23 Anyone who listens to the word but does not do what it says is like someone who looks at his face in a mirror 24 and, after looking at himself, goes away and immediately forgets what he looks like. 25 But whoever looks intently into the perfect law that gives freedom, and continues in it—not forgetting what they have heard, but doing it—they will be blessed in what they do. 26 Those who consider themselves religious and yet do not keep a tight rein on their tongues deceive themselves, and their religion is worthless."
    - Thoughts:

Chapter 6: Community

After I had taken a gap year, I entered into my first year at Lock Haven University. I was nervous and excited. I was fresh out of ministry school, where theology and practical ministry were drilled into me. I couldn't wait to share Jesus to others and be an example in a secular college. I was ready and willing to go and do what God wanted me to do! However, I was three hours from home, and I didn't know anybody yet. At the beginning of school, I would watch my home church online, because I didn't know where to go. I went to a couple different churches, but I didn't really meet anyone, and I still felt alone and uncomfortable.

On top of this, my roommates were very into partying. I had told them that I didn't drink or party, and they were ok with that at first. However, they urged me a couple times to go out with them and I did. Slowly, I saw myself getting more and more comfortable with the idea of going out. I began to listen to the same trashy music I used to like. I got more comfortable with sin than I had been in a while, and I almost didn't even realize it was happening. Here I was, getting into old habits, when my "mission" was to share Jesus.

One day I went to a new church, and was quickly welcomed by the "college group" leader. She introduced me to the other girls and I felt connections right away. Since then, I have been attending Bible studies on campus as well as other ministries. I realized that I *needed* community. Having a Christian community is not designed to make a Christian group isolated from non-Christians. Having a Christian community around you is necessary for your own faith. This doesn't mean you have to spend 100% of your time around your Christian friends. However, it does mean building relationships with those who have the same faith as you. As it says in 1 Corinthians 12, we are one body. We work *together*. We have the Holy Spirit, but we have to have other Christians around us, or we will fall into old sin. We need people to hold us accountable, build us up, and talk with us.

Having community includes serving together and doing life together. If you are constantly around those who aren't Christians, you will struggle. Soon, you will start to fall into sin and begin to be desensitized to it. With no Christian community, you will not grow. You will be heavily influenced by others, instead of being built up by others. There is nothing wrong with having friends who aren't Christians! However, there needs to be a balance. You need mentors and peers who have the same (or very similar) beliefs as you. Seek out opportunities to get into community with others.

Finding a community will usually not be easy! I was very intimidated and nervous going to my first Bible study. It took a couple weeks, if not the whole semester, for me to feel comfortable. Now, I am so thankful that I pushed through the awkward times and developed relationships with the girls in my Bible study! We get to talk, go to church together, hang out together, share prayer requests and pray together, etc! Finding a Christian community is probably one of the most impactful things that happened to me my first semester.

  If you feel like you don't have a community, you should pray that God would give you one. He will hear your prayer and send someone your way! Keep in mind, though, that you have to also be willing to go outside your comfort zone and actively find a community. It is easy to sit around and do nothing about it, but then nothing will happen! You have to choose to find other people and develop relationships with others. It may be challenging, but it is so worth it! Consider 5 things that community brings: community brings encouragement, community is life-giving, community attracts the Holy Spirit, community brings love, and community brings joy! We are not to live isolated...especially not isolated in our beliefs.

- Do you have anyone in your life that encourages you and helps you in your walk with Christ?

- If you don't have a community now, what steps do you plan to take to find one?

- List some ways that a community would be beneficial in your life.

- Galatians 6:2, "Carry each other's burdens, and in this way you will fulfill the law of Christ."
    - Thoughts:

- Proverbs 27:17, "As iron sharpens iron, so one person sharpens another."
    - Thoughts:

- Matthew 18:20, "For where two or three gather in my name, there am I with them."
    - Thoughts:

- Romans 12:5, "so in Christ we, though many, form one body, and each member belongs to all the others."
    - Thoughts:

- Romans 1:11-12, "I long to see you so that I may impart to you some spiritual gift to make you strong—that is, that you and I may be mutually encouraged by each other's faith."
  - Thoughts:

- John 15:12-13, "My command is this: Love each other as I have loved you. Greater love has no one than this: to lay down one's life for one's friends."
  - Thoughts:

- Hebrews 10:24-25, "And let us consider how we may spur one another on toward love and good deeds, not giving up meeting together, as some are in the habit of doing, but encouraging one another—and all the more as you see the Day approaching."
  - Thoughts:

- 1 Peter 2:9-10, "But you are a chosen people, a royal priesthood, a holy nation, God's special possession, that you may declare the praises of him who called you out of darkness into his wonderful light. Once you were not a people, but now you are the people of God; once you had not received mercy, but now you have received mercy."
  - Thoughts:

- 1 Corinthians 12:25-27, "so that there should be no division in the body, but that its parts should have equal concern for each other. If one part suffers, every part suffers with it; if one part is honored, every part rejoices with it. Now you are the body of Christ, and each one of you is a part of it."
  - Thoughts:

- 1 Peter 4:8-11, "Above all, love each other deeply, because love covers over a multitude of sins. Offer hospitality to one another without grumbling. Each of you should use whatever gift you have received to serve others, as faithful stewards of God's grace in its various forms. If anyone speaks, they should do so as one who speaks the very words of God. If anyone serves, they should do so with the strength God provides, so that in all things God may be praised through Jesus Christ. To him be the glory and the power for ever and ever. Amen."
  - Thoughts:

- Ecclesiastes 4:9-12, "Two are better than one, because they have a good return for their labor: If either of them falls down, one can help the other up. But pity anyone who falls and has no one to help them up. Also, if two lie down together, they will keep warm. But how can one keep warm alone? Though one may be overpowered, two can defend themselves. A cord of three strands is not quickly broken."
  - Thoughts:

- Acts 2:44-47, "All the believers were together and had everything in common. They sold property and possessions to give to anyone who had need. Every day they continued to meet together in the temple courts. They broke bread in their homes and ate together with glad and sincere hearts, praising God and enjoying the favor of all the people. And the Lord added to their number daily those who were being saved."
  - Thoughts:

Chapter 7: Perseverance

Going "against the grain" can be very difficult at times. It's hard to focus on doing things differently. It gets difficult to refrain from acting like everyone else, and to maintain a positive attitude. It can be difficult to remind yourself to confide in the Lord daily and pray. Life gets busy. It's hard to think of putting a lot of energy into your spiritual life when the rest of your life seems out of control.

There will be times in our lives where we are overwhelmed and stressed, and there will be times when we are peaceful and overjoyed. Each day, we go through ups and downs. Some days, we will mess up. Other days, we will do great and accomplish everything we desired to accomplish. Some days, we will feel intimately close to God, and other days we will question if He is even listening.

Why Persevere?

Perseverance produces faith. When we remain strong in God, we develop more faith in Him. We get the opportunity to see Him work in amazing ways. We could not see a miracle in our lives if there was not an opportunity for God to work. Perseverance in hard times sometimes allows us to see His working more clearly. Perseverance also develops our spiritual strength. When we trust God in the dark times, we learn more and more to trust Him at every time in our lives.

It is important to remind yourself that God is present at *all times.* God does not work when you are feeling Him. He works continually. Whether you "feel" Him or not, God is always there. God is not an experience...He is the almighty, all-powerful, ever-present God. God is also a God who does not lie. When God says that He will NEVER leave you, or NEVER forsake you (Deuteronomy 31:6), He means just that.

God is always there

Think about your closest loved one. Think about when you are with them and you feel peace and love. Maybe having a hug from a loved one is comforting--you feel secure in their arms. Spending time with a loved one is important to your relationship, and it is beneficial. Your loved one could be anyone from your mom or dad, to your brother or sister, spouse, grandparent, etc. When you get busy, you spend less time with your loved one. When you are stressed, you could also spend less time with your loved one. Perhaps they offer you a hug and you don't accept it. Or, perhaps, you are mad at your situation and take your aggression out on them. Just because you are "busy" or going through a tough time doesn't mean that your loved one isn't *there.* Your loved one didn't disappear or cease to love you. Instead, situations got between your relationship.

God is also your loved one. Sometimes you feel Him closely. You feel His "hug" and His peace and love. Other times, you get caught up in life and spend time away from Him. You might go through challenging circumstances and blame God. You may place your anger on God and yell at Him. However, that does not change the fact that God is *there*. Your circumstances may change, but God remains the same. He is always there for you, and He will NEVER leave you!

Keeping this in mind, we should persevere in our faith. No matter what the circumstance of our life may be, we need to continue to follow God and reach out to Him. We need to spend time in the Word, and keep in contact with our Christian community. We need to focus our attention on what is truly important. Distraction from God is a tool the enemy can use. Being overwhelmed with a busy schedule can get you very distracted from God, and the true joy and peace that is found only in Him. When you are able to, cut out things from your schedule that may be overwhelming to you. If this is not an option in your situation, change your focus. Persevere in the hard times, and look to God at all times. Take care of your body, your mind, and your soul. Do not get burdened by your situations, but at all times cast your cares on the Lord.

- What are some challenges you are going through now?

- Are you spending enough time with God? Do you feel that you only need God at certain times, instead of all the time?

- Have you ever lashed out at God for something? Have you ever cried out to God?

- What areas of your life are the hardest in which to persevere right now? How can you encourage yourself, and find others to encourage you, as well?

- Deuteronomy 31:6, "Be strong and courageous. Do not be afraid or terrified because of them, for the Lord your God goes with you; he will never leave you nor forsake you."
  - Thoughts:

- Colossians 1:11-12, "being strengthened with all power according to his glorious might so that you may have great endurance and patience, and giving joyful thanks to the Father, who has qualified you to share in the inheritance of his holy people in the kingdom of light."
    - Thoughts:

- James 1:12, "Blessed is the one who perseveres under trial because, having stood the test, that person will receive the crown of life that the Lord has promised to those who love him."
    - Thoughts:

- 2 Thessalonians 3:13, "And as for you, brothers and sisters, never tire of doing what is good."
    - Thoughts:

- Proverbs 3:5-6, "Trust in the Lord with all your heart and lean not on your own understanding; in all your ways submit to him, and he will make your paths straight"
  - Thoughts:

- Ecclesiastes 9:11, "I have seen something else under the sun: The race is not to the swift or the battle to the strong, nor does food come to the wise or wealth to the brilliant or favor to the learned; but time and chance happen to them all."
  - Thoughts:

- Luke 21:19, "Stand firm, and you will win life."
  - Thoughts:

Chapter 8: Boldness

The Bible tells us time and time again how important it is to share our faith and witness to others. We are to go out and make disciples, and share the good news of Jesus to everyone. If you're anything like me, this can be rather challenging because you are not naturally bold. Being bold does not mean you have to go into a crowded room and start quoting scripture at the top of your lungs. Being bold means being willing to take risks, to be confident, and to have courage.

What Does Boldness Look Like for Me?

Depending on who you are, being bold can look differently. If you are a naturally outgoing person, an example of being bold would be something that pushes you out of your comfort zone. Perhaps you are a natural evangelist--you can easily talk to anyone about anything and have no problem being the center of attention. God may use this ability to boldly share your beliefs with others in ways that certain people can't.

If being in the spotlight or in front of a crowd isn't your thing, that doesn't mean you can't be bold. God will use what He has given you, no matter who you are. Maybe being bold for you looks like talking to someone who everyone else ignores. Maybe it means telling one of your friends about Jesus. Or, it could be serving others in a way that stretches your faith.

Know Your Stuff

Whatever boldness may look like in your life, we are called to be bold. We are to have courage and be confident in what we believe in. Some ways to be extra confident in your beliefs are to research theology and apologetics. You may want to explore various books that talk about common arguments against Christianity and how to respond to them. You should know *why* you believe what you believe, and be prepared to talk about it. You should also know how to share the Gospel in a simple way.

Having all of these things "in your belt" will make you more confident and willing to be bold. Your boldness and efforts will be rewarded! Not only will God be proud of you, but you will be proud of yourself. You will grow more and more comfortable with stepping out of your comfort zone, and learning to depend on the Holy Spirit for strength and guidance.

Don't Let the Devil Get'cha!

Be on your guard when you begin to act boldly. The devil will sneak lies into your mind like "you can't do that," "you aren't good at that," "did you see the way those people looked at you? They must think you're totally crazy," "someone else other than you would be better at this," etc. Do not let these thoughts get to your head. They are lies from the enemy that are meant to discourage you. With God, all things are possible...even things that you may have thought you could never do. Believing the lies of the enemy will discourage you and you will not grow in faith. When thoughts cause you to doubt yourself, remember who *God* has made you to be. Remember that He wants to work through you. It may take time, but through focus and perseverance, God will use you to make a significant impact. Do not forget that the little things make a huge difference. Being bold to say "hello" to someone can be a step in the right direction! Being bold to hold your tongue when gossip is occurring is honoring God. It doesn't matter who you are, God WILL use you!

- What is one area in your life that you want to be more bold in? How are you going to challenge yourself to be bold in this area?

- In what ways would being bold encourage you in your faith, as well as those around you?

- What are you most afraid about when it comes to being bold? Do you think that God is in control, even beyond what you are afraid of (hint: He is!)?

- Acts 28:31, "Proclaiming the kingdom of God and teaching about the Lord Jesus Christ with all boldness and without hindrance."
  - Thoughts:

- Proverbs 28:1, "The wicked flee when no one pursues, but the righteous are bold as a lion."
  - Thoughts:

- Hebrews 13:6, "So we can confidently say, "The Lord is my helper; I will not fear; what can man do to me?"
  - Thoughts:

- Joshua 1:9, "Have I not commanded you? Be strong and courageous. Do not be frightened, and do not be dismayed, for the Lord your God is with you wherever you go."
  - Thoughts:

- 2 Timothy 1:6-7, "For this reason I remind you to fan into flame the gift of God, which is in you through the laying on of my hands, for God gave us a spirit not of fear but of power and love and self-control."
  - ○ Thoughts:

- Romans 12:1-2, "I appeal to you therefore, brothers, by the mercies of God, to present your bodies as a living sacrifice, holy and acceptable to God, which is your spiritual worship. Do not be conformed to this world, but be transformed by the renewal of your mind, that by testing you may discern what is the will of God, what is good and acceptable and perfect."
  - ○ Thoughts:

- Acts 4:28-29, "But everything they did was determined beforehand according to your will. And now, O Lord, hear their threats, and give us, your servants, great boldness in preaching your word."
  - ○ Thoughts:

- Ephesians 6:19-20, "And pray for me, too. Ask God to give me the right words so I can boldly explain God's mysterious plan that the Good News is for Jews and Gentiles alike. I am in chains now, still preaching this message as God's ambassador. So pray that I will keep on speaking boldly for him, as I should."
  - Thoughts:

- Acts 4:13, "The members of the council were amazed when they saw the boldness of Peter and John, for they could see that they were ordinary men with no special training in the Scriptures. They also recognized them as men who had been with Jesus."
  - Thoughts:

- Psalm 27:14 "Wait on the Lord. Be courageous, and he will strengthen your heart. Wait on the Lord!"
  - Thoughts:

- Romans 8:31, "What, then, shall we say in response to these things? If God is for us, who can be against us?"
  - Thoughts:

Chapter 9: Love the Lord Your God

Love is a beautiful thing. We are called to love one another, regardless of belief, looks, size, race, background, etc. We should love people unconditionally and know that each person is a son and a daughter of God. Our love should be contagious and amazing. Our love that we display for others should be inspiring and obvious. Though we may not particularly like the habits of some people, and though we may not support what they do, that does not mean that we should not *love* them. We need to encourage others, serve others, be kind to others, and share the Gospel with others. All of this must be done out of genuine love.

How can we get this love? How do we learn to love other people in the same way that Christ first loved us? It starts by truly knowing God. The more that you learn about God, His mercy, His love, His faithfulness, and His sacrifice, the more that you will love Him. The Bible describes God as the vine, and we are the branches (John 15:5). We grow from Him, but we have to be connected to Him. We also have to be connected to Him if we want to continue to grow and bear fruit. To truly love others, we have to understand what true love looks like.

John 15 describes this perfectly, "I am the true vine, and my Father is the gardener. 2 He cuts off every branch in me that bears no fruit, while every branch that does bear fruit he prunes so that it will be even more fruitful. 3 You are already clean because of the word I have spoken to you. 4 Remain in me, as I also remain in you. No branch can bear fruit by itself; it must remain in the vine. Neither can you bear fruit unless you remain in me. 5 "I am the vine; you are the branches. If you remain in me and I in you, you will bear much fruit; apart from me you can do nothing. 6 If you do not remain in me, you are like a branch that is thrown away and withers; such branches are picked up, thrown into the fire and burned. 7 If you remain in me and my words remain in you, ask whatever you wish, and it will be done for you. 8 This is to my Father's glory, that you bear much fruit, showing yourselves to be my disciples. 9 "As the Father has loved me, so have I loved you. Now remain in my love. 10 If you keep my commands, you will remain in my love, just as I have kept my Father's commands and remain in his love. 11 I have told you this so that my joy may be in you and that your joy may be complete. 12 My command is this: Love each other as I have loved you. 13 Greater love has no one than this: to lay down one's life for one's friends. 14 You are my friends if you do what I command. 15 I no longer call you servants, because a servant does not know his master's business. Instead, I have called you friends, for everything that I learned from my Father I have made known to you. 16 You did not choose me, but I chose you and appointed you so that you might go and bear fruit—fruit that will last—and so that whatever you ask in my name the Father will give you. 17 This is my command: Love each other."

God is the perfect Father. He is always right, and He disciplines out of love. He is a father that will never leave, and will always love you. He is a graceful father, and He is interested in every aspect of your life. He is a wise father, and He will give you wisdom and understanding. He is a generous father, a strong father, a protective father, a Holy father, and a forgiving father. How great is it that we can have a personal relationship with our Lord...the one who created the earth and everything in it! We can talk to Him and learn from Him. We can love Him, and He loves us back. He is real and He is living. He is extending out His arms to show you love and to show you grace!

Accepting His love is an important step to learning to love others. Each person around you is created by God, and He loves each and every one of His children. If only all of them knew this! So, until those around us accept Christ, it is our duty to exemplify the love of God. You are not perfect, so you may not be like this all of the time, but you will grow. As you continue to push yourself deeper in your faith and your relationship with God, your love will grow, too. The Holy Spirit will fill you and you will do things that others cannot. You will stand up for what is right, you will love unconditionally, you will be bold and be focused, you will withstand opposition, you will be a leader, you will display the fruit of the Spirit, and you will do what God has called you to do. What an exciting life it is to be walking with God!

- Do you have trouble loving others now, or is it easy? How can you show your love to others more?

- Is your love "selective?" Meaning, you choose to love certain people but not others? How can you work on loving *everyone?*

- How can you demonstrate love to those who may be criticizing you or hating you?

- How did Jesus model love?

- Romans 12:9-16, "Love must be sincere. Hate what is evil; cling to what is good. Be devoted to one another in love. Honor one another above yourselves. Never be lacking in zeal, but keep your spiritual fervor, serving the Lord. Be joyful in hope, patient in affliction, faithful in prayer. Share with the Lord's people who are in need. Practice hospitality. Bless those who persecute you; bless and do not curse. Rejoice with those who rejoice; mourn with those who mourn. Live in harmony with one another."
  - Thoughts:

- Colossians 3:12-14, "You are the people of God; he loved you and chose you for his own. So then, you must clothe yourselves with compassion, kindness, humility, gentleness, and patience. Be tolerant with one another and forgive one another whenever any of you has a complaint against someone else. You must forgive one another just as the Lord has forgiven you. And to all these qualities add love, which binds all things together in perfect unity."
  - Thoughts:

- 1 John 4:7, "Dear friends, let us love one another, for love comes from God."
  - Thoughts:

- 1 John 4:9-11, "This is how God showed his love among us: He sent his one and only Son into the world that we might live through him. This is love: not that we loved God, but that he loved us and sent his Son as an atoning sacrifice for our sins. Dear friends, since God so loved us, we also ought to love one another."
  - Thoughts:

- 1 John 4:18-19, "There is no fear in love. But perfect love drives out fear, because fear has to do with punishment. The one who fears is not made perfect in love. We love because he first loved us."
    - Thoughts:

- Proverbs 4:23, "Above all else, guard your heart, for everything you do flows from it."
    - Thoughts:

- 1 Corinthians 13:4-8, "Love is patient, love is kind. It does not envy, it does not boast, it is not proud. It does not dishonor others, it is not self-seeking, it is not easily angered, it keeps no record of wrongs. Love does not delight in evil but rejoices with the truth. It always protects, always trusts, always hopes, always perseveres."
    - Thoughts:

Notes

Notes

Made in United States
Orlando, FL
05 February 2022